Plate 1 WINTER... *Wind blown snow forms a cornice along Mt. Baldy's West Ridge. February 1979.*

Plate 2 SPRING...At Tanners Flat, delicate shades of green herald the end of winter. May 1985.

Plate 3 SUMMER...*Wildflowers cover an alp below the Emerald
Cirque on Mount Timpanogos. July 1987.*

Plate 4 AUTUMN...*Reflections in the pond at Cascade Springs. October 1984.*

Introduction

If you don't yet acknowledge photography as art, I suggest you spend some time examining the stunning mountain photography John Barstow has assembled in Wasatch Silhouette. On page after page photographic art triumphs over mere camera technology. In one image of mountain and flowers, for example, the viewer is taken from darkened roots in the foreground to exquisite, bright blossoms, an alpine cirque, a distant and forbidding peak, and finally to clouds and sunburst. One can imagine the photographer lying on his stomach, straining for just the right angle, waiting for the precise moment of anticipated light.

This is a work of photographic autobiography. It represents the dedication of nearly half John's life to the Wasatch Mountains, as a lodge employee, ski patrolman, hiker and climber. Following the seasons from winter to summer and back, Wasatch Silhouette meanders through the mountains as John has, camera in hand.

John's photographs of rock and ice climbers practicing their craft are already well known. One, included in this book, of an intrepid woman ascending a frozen waterfall, makes the viewer wonder where the photographer can have stood. The camera seems to float, suspended above the climber. Such unusual situations and perspectives are recurrent elements in these images. A view of the southern Little Cottonwood ridge appears to have been taken from a hovering helicopter. In reality, it was captured with a telescopic lens from a valley parking lot. Other remarkable photos freeze the firing of an avalanche control gun and the release of a massive slide from the flank of the American Fork Twin Peaks.

But dramatic action and novel perspective are kept company here by an obvious sensitivity to the mountains' subtly changing moods. Images in golden tones, of stringy gray clouds and swirling snow leave the viewer with a sense of how mountains and light interact on the emulsion of the photographer's eye.

If we bring to this viewing an effort of our own, to recall our own stored images of these mountains, and the feelings they inspired, then we can share here the wondrous and fulfilling experience of two artists meeting—the one in our mind's eye, and the other on these pages.

Ted Wilson

Mr. Wilson has spent many of his own years in the mountains of the Wasatch Front. He is a skier, hiker and climber with a long list of first ascents in these peaks. Ted was elected mayor of Salt Lake City three times, and currently serves as Director of the Hinckley Institute of Politics at the University of Utah.

Plate 5 *The crisp light of an autumn evening on High Rustler and Mount Baldy, Alta. October 1989.*

Plate 6 *Hoar frost and the first snows of winter etch the ridges of Little Cottonwood. October 1984.*

I began work on Wasatch Silhouette in the summer of 1985. Some of the photographs reproduced here were made as recently as June 1990. Others go back as far as 1972, and the first roll of film through the first (of many) Nikon cameras. Photography is neither experience nor life…but it can be a reflection of the experience of life. Eighteen years of my life are reflected here. That's a lot of film under the bridge and countless good friends come and gone. Many more of them are part of this book than appear on these very few pages.

John Barstow *June,* 1990

Photography: John M. Barstow
Design & production: Bill Tobey
Introduction by Ted Wilson
Printed in Hong Kong by
Everbest Printing Co., Ltd./Asiaprint

Signed original prints of the photographs
reproduced in this book are available from:
John Barstow
P.O. Box 646
Sandy, Utah 84091
(801) 943-8316

WASATCH SILHOUETTE

Photographs By John Barstow

Plate 7 *The last rays of Sunset on Lone Peak. May 1990.*

Plate 8 *A winter's day dawn in Little Cottonwood Canyon. February 1976.*

Plate 9 *Sunrise above Mineral Basin. March 1978.*

Plate 10 *Bob Black in deep, deep powder on the north end of Anderson's Hill. April 1978.*

Plate 11 *An island in a sea of clouds…the ridge from Twin Peaks to Mount Superior. January 1979.*

Plate 12 *Avalanche control team along the ridge west of Hidden Peak. February 1976.*

Plate 13 *Early morning shooting, the Peruvian Ridge gun at Snowbird. March 1979.*

Plates 14-17 *A shot from the ridge triggers a massive avalanche on the East Face of Twin Peaks. December 1976.*

Plate 18 *At sunrise, ice crystals in the air form a sun dog below the cloud layer. January 1976.*

Plate 19 *"Elder Velvet" shredding the Primrose Path. April 1978.*

Plate 20 *Strong winds and scoured snow in Baldy's Bowl. January 1979.*

Plate 22 *Snowbird ski patrollers check slope stability above the Peruvian Cirque. March 1979.*

Plate 23 *Jon Stratton and Rocky at Joint Point, along the White Pine ridge. March 1976.*

Plate 21 *An exploding hand charge results in slope failure. April 1977.*

Plate 24 *Rick Mandahl making turns on Anderson's Hill. April 1978.*

Plate 25 *Randy Trover, early morning on Silver Fox. March 1977.*

Plate 26 *Opposite: Slivers of light in Maybird Gulch...Carol Petrelli. February 1988.*

Plate 27 *Above: Jimmy Collinson airborn on Regulator Johnson. March 1988.*

Plate 28 *Little Cloud...sunburst and clearing storm. February 1979.*

Plate 29 *Steve Goldsmith in the forest behind the Gad II lift shack.*
January 1979.

Plate 30 *Carl Gotland on Baldy Shoulder. February 1987.*

Plate 31 *Wind whipped snow on upper Chip's Run. January 1979.*

Plate 32 *Approaching storm at the mouth of Little Cottonwood. March 1977.*

Plate 33 *Moods of the Pfeifferhorn. February 1976.*

Plate 34 *February 1977*

Plate 35 *February 1978*

Plate 36 *February 1979*

Plate 37 - 38 *Elk at winters rest in Blacksmith's Fork Canyon. February 1990.*

Plate 39 Mountain goat, Wasatch silhouette. July 1977.

Plate 40 *Les Ellison on a very bold ice climb near the mouth of Provo Canyon. March 1984.*

Plate 41 *Mugs Stump on Bridalveil Falls, Provo Canyon. December 1986.*

Plate 42 *Carol Petrelli in Santaquin Canyon, high on the north
side of Mount Nebo. February 1988.*

Plate 43 *Compact snow makes trail breaking easy for Karen Aldous. Big Cottonwood Canyon. December 1984.*

Plate 44 *Spring corn snow near the top of the Tanners slide path. Skier: Jimmy Collinson. May 1987.*

Plate 45 *Top left: Powder Ridge at Snow Basin. Skier:*
Susan Waite. February 1989.

Plate 47 *Bottom left: Jon Turk, Maybird Gulch. December 1985.*

Plate 46 *Top right: James Garrett on White Pine corn. April 1987.*

Plate 48 *Bottom right: Christine Seashore in Broads Fork.*
January 1988.

Plate 49 *Big Cottonwood Canyon on a late spring day. May 1983.*

Plate 50 *Roody the Hood skiing soft avalanche debris in the Peruvian Cirque. February 1984.*

Plate 51 *Gentle sweep of the cornice along White Pine's east ridge. January 1979.*

Plate 52 *Opposite: At the end of a very cold day the soft glow of winter sunset on Grizzly Gulch. January 1985.*

Plate 53 *Above: Sunset…Storm Mountain. March 1987.*

Plate 54 *The great north faces of the Wasatch Front: Mount Olympus and the Twin Peaks. March 1985.*

Plate 55 *Sunset, Heber Valley. January 1986.*

Plate 56 *Star trails in the night sky above my camp near Lone Peak. April 1987.*

Plate 57 *A spring day and corn snow in the Baldy Chutes. June 1987.*

Plate 58 *A family of mountain goats in the Emerald Cirque of Mount Timpanogos. July 1987.*

Plate 59 *Springtime at Bridalveil Falls, Provo Canyon. May 1984.*

Plate 60 *Mid-summer along the Timpanogos trail. July 1987.*

Plate 61

Plate 62

Plate 63 *The Sundial reflected in Lake Blanche, near the head of Mill B Canyon. May 1984.*

Plate 64 *Columbine bloom in Albion Basin, below Devil's Castle. August 1984.*

Plate 65 *The tranquility of Cecret Lake, Alta. August 1984.*

Plate 66 *A carpet of wildflowers above the town of Alta. August 1984.*

Plate 67 *The Salt Lake Twin Peaks reflected in Red Pine Lake. September 1983.*

Plate 68 *Left: Bald eagle in the woods near Sundance.
May 1984.*

Plate 69 *Above: Mule deer on the slopes of Snowbird.
September 1989.*

Plate 70 *Alpine Buttercups along the west ridge of the Pfeifferhorn. July 1982.*

Plate 71 *Summer is a fleeting and delicate thing high in the Lone Peak Cirque. August 1983.*

Plate 72 *Julie Gustin rock climbing on ''The Coffin'' in Little*
Cottonwood Canyon. June 1990.

Plate 73 *Doug Heinrich on Little Cottonwood's "The Big Neon Glitter." May 1990.*

Plate 74 *Stuart Ruckman on a very difficult Big Cottonwood route, "The Enemy Within." June 1990.*

Plate 75 *A late summer storm brings snow to lower Big Cottonwood Canyon. September 1983.*

Plate 76   Left: Overlooking Hogum Fork, high up in
Little Cottonwood Canyon. August 1983.

Plate 77   Above: A rock climber rappels in the face of an
afternoon storm. Little Cottonwood Canyon.
August 1983.

Plate 78 *Storm clouds and summer sunset on the Twin Peaks. July 1984.*

Plate 79 *The soft hues of alpenglow reflected on the walls of Thunder Mountain and Bells Canyon. August 1984.*

Plate 80 *Sunset above Alta and Mount Superior. September 1989.*

Plate 81 *The crescent moon rising over Twin Peaks. July 1984.*

Plate 82 *Aspen leaves show the flicker of late summer; a trace of new snow on Mount Baldy. September 1972.*

Plate 83 *A brilliant summer afternoon along the high ridges of Hogum Fork. September 1983.*

Plate 84 *Autumn Aloft, Park City. September 1989.*

Plate 86 *Calf roping at Kamas, Utah. July 1984.*

Plate 85 *Small town rodeo, saddle bronc rider, Morgan, Utah. June 1984.*

Plate 87 *Opposite: Golden aspens make a strong statement for change near the bottom of Red Pine. October 1983.*

Plate 88 *Above: Early snows high on the north peak of Mount Timpanogos etch the sky on a clear autumn day. October 1984.*

Plate 89 *Above: A gentle cascade on the American Fork River below the Alpine Loop. October 1983.*

Plate 90 *Right: Rushing water at Cascade Springs. October 1984.*

Plate 91 *Left: A vision from an earlier time, probably carved by an isolated Basque shepherd along the Skyline Trail. September 1981.*

Plate 92 *Below: Sheep camp in late autumn on the flank of Mount Timpanogos. October 1984.*

Plate 93 *A quiet afternoon along the Provo River. October 1984.*

Plate 94 *Bridalveil Falls. October 1984.*

Plate 95 *Early season color change in American Fork Canyon.*
September 1981.

Plate 96 *Lower Gad Valley near Little Cottonwood Creek.*
October 1983.

Plate 97 *The northwest face of Mount Olympus. October 1986.*

Plate 98   *Above: Lazy daze before winter. A mountain goat on Devil's Castle. November 1976.*

Plate 99   *Right: Seasons change at Little Pine slide area. October 1984.*

Plate 100   *Opposite: Devil's Castle dusted with late summer snow. September 1989.*

Plate 101 *The Dog's Tooth, above the North Fork of Deaf Smith Canyon. October 1983.*

Plate 102 *A quiet autumn evening along the trail to Scott's Pass, near Brighton ski area. October 1983.*

Plate 103 *Calm before the storm. Late summer in American Fork. October 1984.*

Plate 104 *Sunrise flight. Mallard ducks leaving the Bear River. November 1980.*

Plate 105 *Autumn gold reflected in the beaver pond at Cascade Springs. October 1984.*

Plate 106 Above: *Dawn broke over Locomotive Springs and the bay was full of ducks. They heard my camera and they were gone. November 1985.*

Plate 107 Opposite: *Aspen leaves and snow, both newly fallen. November 1984.*

Plate 108 *Headin' south. Honkers over Willard Bay. November 1980.*

Plate 109 *Carved by glaciers and accented with early winter snow…Little Cottonwood Canyon. October 1984.*

Plate 110 *Above: Sunset over Little Cottonwood Canyon. July 1972.*

Plate 111 *Opposite: Alpenglow and the full moon. April 1985.*

Plate 112 *Elk in snow storm...Winter 1990.*